Whispered Verities

Ruminations & Poems

Sara B. Dower

Made with ❤ on the BookLeaf Publishing Platform
www.bookleafpub.in
www.bookleafpub.com

Dedication

To all who have a mind that rarely quiets itself and feels everything all of the time.

To Ava and Finley for inspiring me every day and convincing me to follow my heart.

It belongs to you forever.

Preface

From the moment I read a poem that spoke to me poetry became a refuge. When I penned my first poems as a teenager, I found solace. It is a form of expression that gives an unapologetic voice to thoughts that swirl around my mind. Poetry invites introspection and reflection. It allows us to embrace joy, sorrow, love, and loss in unique ways. Reading it feeds my soul. Writing it lets me savor the beautiful experiences I want to treasure and release the emotions that are not serving me. It is a safe space in a world that has too few of those.

This collection touches on different forms of love and loss and the whispered thoughts that help me navigate both.

Acknowledgements

Thank you, Bill, Ava, and Finley for knowing that writing is a part of me whether I publish a darn thing or not.

Mom and Dad, thank you for supporting my daydreams for some time now.

Marian, thank you for encouraging me. I appreciate you.

Jessica, if it were not for you this book would not exist. You told me to just go for it. Thank you for cheering me on and keeping me on track.

Rachel Calabrese, thank you for your constant encouragement and telling me not to give up on what I love.

Hillary, I appreciate your support of my random social media posts, writing challenges, and the like, and for being solid technical support when my computer was moody.

Mandi, with a sad loss came inspiration and a fire was ignited. You are my stargazer friend for eternity.

Gavin, thank you for your kind, discreet support.

BookLeaf Publishing, thank you for making it possible for me to get my feet wet and publish this mixed bag of poetry.

Tether

Please
hold my hand
while I sleep
and tether me
to this world.

I fear I'll dream
of wonderous things
and not want to
return.

Missing You

My phone stopped
recognizing your name
and tries to
autocorrect it.
A digital reminder
life's not the same,
but how could I ever
expect that?
I need you to know
you're still with me.
I think of you each day.
At times a noise
will sound like you
and take my breath away.
I really believe
I will see you again.
I'm not sure
by what means.
Until that time
keep visiting me
in my sweetest dreams.

With You

At the library
by the sea
an enchanted wood
or art gallery.

In the car
music plays
Fade Into You
Dance Hall Days.

Silent or musing
whatever will do
anytime
anywhere
when I'm with you.

Ember

I was afraid of your love
and fought it,
craving it nonetheless.

A spark was enough
to ignite us
despite the
resounding protests.

Wild and free
we never could be
and even less can
we be now.

Remember my voice
as I shall yours,
I am stamping
the ember out.

Early Morning

A band of pale orange
through tree silhouettes.
The brightest star's fringe
is my favorite vignette.

So quiet and still,
this breathtaking view
just past my sill
stirs thoughts of you.

A Simple Day

Pockets of rain.
Patches of blue.
A simple day
is made
wondrous
with you.

Over

You took so much
but not everything.
I would have
given you more.
I am relieved
it ended
but we forgot
to lock the door.

Pace

Just as leaves turn
from green to red
then fall upon
the ground we tread
emotions also
shift and sway with
the colorful rhythms
of each new day.

For better or worse
with every season
my body reacts
without rhyme or reason.

Are attempts to control it
a noble cause or
a perilous plan
with inherent flaws?

Moving through
every ebb and flow
armed with knowledge
of how it could go.

Look for the silver
remembering grace
keep an auspicious hope
for upcoming days.

Retraction

Love poems for him
were elegies.
Love poems for you
are palinodes.
You are a salve
on my shredded heart.
Now it can beat
with yours.

Knowing Me

No one knows
my heart like you.
From its darkness
to its damn virtue.
My faults are
your fire.
My bliss
your desire.
Just a smirk
or passing glance
is all it takes
to fuel romance.

Tiresome

I wish that I could
quiet my mind
to think about
less than five
things at a time.

The weariness
that comes
from ceaseless
reeling
leaves me exhausted
and numb of all
feeling.

That in turn
causes
greater despair
though I tell myself
I am not being fair.

Counteracting self-talk
is a job in itself
which squanders
my time

and weakens
my health.

I write these
thoughts down
and chuckle a bit.
Finding humor in angst
is a much better fit.

Looking Back

Looking back,
there are things I
wish I could change.

The slamming doors.
The maddening rage.

Looking back,
what would I do?
Would I engage?

Say it's okay and keep
holding my tongue
while knowing inside
I'm not the one?

Looking back,
I close the door softly.
What's done is done.

No Last Words

No last words.
No goodbyes.
I hug you as
tears stream.
Losing you
all over again
each time I wake
from dreams.

Personal Protest

Are we to move on
from losing you just
because you are at rest?
I know this may be selfish.
Call it a personal protest.

The cruel comfort
of your absence
is you are no longer in pain,
but the cost of such a solace
is not seeing you again.

Not in this life anyway,
for however long that is.
Hopes to dream of you
at night
have become
a haunting wish.

Seeing you without
the black that
stole you from within
is a gift you grant me
until another day begins.

Cosmic

You say we're
cosmic
when we say
the same thing
at the same time.
We could finish
each other's sentences
even in pantomime.

You know my thoughts
before I speak
and know just what
to say.
Although I feign
annoyance,
I adore you know
me this way.

I read you like
an open book,
you know you
can't deny it,
but if we were
truly cosmic

then why did we
dare defy it?

Unconscious

I am sorry for
the things
I wished
when your
sunken cheek
I last kissed.

In The Park

A chromatic tapestry
against crisp blue
reminds me of the
time in the park
when you
held my hand
while your other hand
clutched your lion.

We walked along
the cobbled path,
beyond the pond,
to the overpass
shaded from the
bright yellow sun.

You talked
enthusiastically
observing nature's
bold beauty,
and I
remained amazed
that you were mine.

Two years had gone by
since you entered
our lives
turning what was mundane
to the sublime.

Just as green tree tops
turn gold and
bright crimson
to remind us the
blue sky is really
quite vibrant.

We walked under
immense oak trees
to crunch the first few
fallen leaves and your
giggle echoed pure joy
throughout the park.

There is nothing like
fresh autumn air
and a kaleidoscope
of colors that dare
to take our warm breath
away.

Eighteen years
have passed since then.
When we walk there now
I am with a friend.
Both enamored by
the beauty that
surrounds us.

Every Autumn

Falling mercury.
Falling leaves.
A crisp image of you
makes my heart cleave.

Tasting the air.
Recalling our kiss
'neath a fiery canopy
piquing our bliss.

Every autumn
I fall for you.
Crazy in love
or besotted fool?

Your Worth

It hurts to see you
not love yourself
or think you aren't
worth more.

My hope is you see
your potential –
that you can walk
through any door.

The years have
bent you
prematurely
but you can
salvage what's ahead.

Cling to the *good* words
said to you
not the enemy
you hear instead.

You are more than
your mistakes or
when your faith is weak.

Can one earn such
devoted love
if they only
deserve critique?

Trust in what I tell you
and allow yourself
to be the simply
remarkable person
other people see.

Courage

You're not
looking for
starlight
but you feel
there is a
spotlight
shining down
on your
every move.

No wonder
you have
stage fright
feeling trapped
and uptight
worried about
who will or
won't approve.

With confident
tenacity
brush off
the insecurity
and focus on

the clarity
you have.

Please
see your path
as I do
and aim
your arrow
to be true
to your passion
and to yourself.

In the end
it's down to
you
and having
love for
what you do
really is
the finest
kind of
wealth.

Adrift

For Mandi

Today I lost my compass.
My navigator is gone.
I also lost my anchor
that always held so strong.
When I need to hold my place
but unsteady is the sea,
how do I keep from drifting
beyond where I should be?

I cannot see my lighthouse
standing firm and true.
In a tempest it stood there
firmly guiding me through.
How will I cross the darkness?
What if a fog appears?
A canvas may surround me,
but my Polaris isn't here.

How will I fare without these?
Together they were one.
I'll hold fast 'til tomorrow
relying on the sun.

www.ingramcontent.com/pod-product-compliance
Lightning Source LLC
LaVergne TN
LVHW010954200726

843509LV00013B/2416